Learning to Write
Narrative
Paragraphs

Frances Purslow

Weigl

CALGARY
www.weigl.com

Published by Weigl Educational Publishers Limited
6325 10 Street SE
Calgary, Alberta, Canada T2H 2Z9

Website: www.weigl.com

Library and Archives Canada Cataloguing in Publication Data

Purslow, Frances
      Narrative paragraphs / Frances Purslow.

ISBN 978-1-55388-434-7 (bound).--ISBN 978-1-55388-435-4 (pbk.)

      1. Narration (Rhetoric)--Juvenile literature. 2. English
language--Paragraphs--Juvenile literature. 3. Composition (Language
arts)--Juvenile literature. I. Title.
PE1439.P87 2008   j808'.042   C2008-901426-X

Printed in the United States of America
1 2 3 4 5 6 7 8 9 0 12 11 10 09 08

Editor: Heather Kissock
Design: Terry Paulhus

Photograph Credits
Every reasonable effort has been made to trace ownership and to obtain permission to reprint copyright material. The publishers would be pleased to have any errors or omissions brought to their attention so that they may be corrected in subsequent printings.

Corbis: page 11; CP Images: pages 9, 10, 12T, 12M, 14, 19 20; Royal BC Museum, BC Archives: page 15 (I-60891); Getty Images: pages 4, 5, 6, 7, 8, 17, 21; Library and Archives Canada: page 13 (C-011299, C-066939, C-066946, C-066943, C-066950); Montreal Star/The Gazette (Montreal): page 12B.

We acknowledge the financial support of the Government of Canada through the Book Publishing Industry Development Program (BPIDP) for our publishing activities.

Table of Contents

Learning about Narrative Paragraphs

A narrative paragraph is a group of sentences that tells what happens, how the action happens, and in what order the events occur. Authors use narrative paragraphs to share a story with readers. A narrative paragraph may be complete by itself, or it may be part of a longer piece of writing.

The following is an example of a narrative paragraph. It tells about an event that happened early in the life of one of Canada's prime ministers, Pierre Elliott Trudeau.

When Pierre and his friend entered school, Pierre was placed in a lower grade than his friend. Pierre asked his father to call the school and have him moved up to the same grade as his friend. As a boy, Pierre was quite shy. His father wanted him to overcome his shyness. Pierre's father told him to fight his own battles. Pierre went to see the principal on his own and was moved into second grade. Pierre learned at a young age that he had to be strong and stand up for himself.

The lesson Pierre learned helped him as a **politician**, and later, as prime minister. To find out more about Pierre's life and accomplishments, take the quiz at **http://schools.hpedsb.on.ca/smood/pm/trudeau.htm**. Use the answers to write a brief paragraph about Pierre.

Following the Action

Frederick Banting was a Canadian doctor and scientist. He helped discover a way to treat **diabetes**. The narrative paragraph below describes the event that made Frederick decide to become a doctor. While reading, follow the action in the story. Look for the words that tell the action.

It was an accident that made Frederick Banting decide to become a doctor. One day, Frederick was walking home from school. He stopped to watch two men fix a roof. Suddenly, the platform the men were standing on crashed to the ground. In a panic, Frederick ran to get a doctor. Later, as he watched the doctor bind the men's wounds, Frederick thought how wonderful it must be to have such skill and knowledge. At that moment, he decided to become a doctor.

Write a short paragraph about an event that helped you make a decision. Then, circle the action words in each of your sentences.

What Are Verbs?

A narrative paragraph requires many action words. Action words are called verbs. A writer uses action words to tell what happened in a story.

The following narrative paragraph describes how Avril Lavigne's musical career was launched. Look for the verbs in the paragraph.

*When Avril was two years old, she began to sing at church. At 11 years of age, she taught herself to play her father's guitar. She also started writing songs. Avril performed at local fairs and talent shows when she was in high school. When she was 16, she travelled to New York City to work with a group of music writers. While there, she met a music producer. He gave her a **contract** to make her first album,* Let Go.

Since the release of *Let Go*, Avril has had a successful music career. For more information on the career of this exciting performer, go to **www.avrillavigne.com**, and click on "About." Make a list of the verbs used to describe Avril's story.

Learning to Use Strong Verbs

The following narrative paragraph explains what happened to Canadian car racing champion Jacques Villeneuve in one race during the 1997 Formula One season.

In 1997, Jacques competed against Michael Shumacher to become the overall racing leader. By the final race of the season, Jacques was behind Michael by one point. Michael was leading for most of the race. On the 48th of 69 laps, Jacques tried to pass Michael. The two cars raced neck and neck for a few seconds. Michael's car glanced off Jacques', but Jacques managed to hold it steady. Michael's car flew into the gravel, and Jacques' stayed on track. Jacques led the race until the final lap, when he was passed by two other drivers. Jacques finished third. This gave him enough points to win the overall title.

What actions took place during the race? The cars "raced," "spun," "glanced," and "flew." These actions are verbs. They are strong verbs that help paint a picture of a thrilling sporting event.

Now, read the following sentence.

Jacques Villeneuve went around the race track at a high speed.

Now replace "went" with a stronger verb. Use a thesaurus to find alternate words for "went." You might replace it with "drove," "travelled," "motored," or "hurtled." What other words can you find?

Finding Transitions

Connecting words, such as "then," "next," and "finally," help show the order of time. These connecting words are called transitions. They connect sentences and show the sequence of events.

The following paragraph tells about Canadian writer Margaret Atwood. Notice the transitions that show the order of time.

*After high school, Margaret studied English at the University of Toronto. By the time she graduated, she had published her first book of poetry and won an award for it. Then, she was accepted into Harvard University in the United States for her **master's degree**. After completing her studies at Harvard, Margaret spent the summer with a friend in England. She also travelled throughout France. In autumn, Margaret returned to Canada, where she became an instructor at the University of British Columbia. The year she spent in Vancouver went well. Margaret enjoyed teaching. She also wrote 14 stories and many new poems, created a **draft** of one novel, and started two others. The following year, Margaret returned to study at Harvard.*

Using Transitions

Look at the route marked on the map. This route, plus the transitions in the sentences below, will help you figure out the correct order of the sentences.

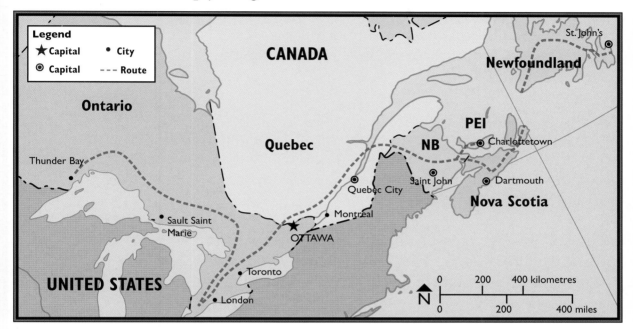

A. On April 12, 1980, Terry Fox began his Marathon of Hope to raise money for cancer research. It was a cold and windy day in St. John's, Newfoundland, when Terry dipped his artificial leg in the Atlantic Ocean.

B. After leaving Toronto, Terry continued his journey through Ontario. His marathon came to an end near Thunder Bay, on September 1, when he became ill with lung cancer. Terry died on June 28, 1981.

C. From Newfoundland, Terry headed south, travelling through Nova Scotia, Prince Edward Island, and New Brunswick.

D. Eighteen days later, on July 11th, Terry arrived in Toronto. More than 10,000 people were on hand at city hall to give him a hero's welcome.

E. Then, he headed into the province of Quebec, reaching Montreal on June 23.

Answers: 1. A 2. C 3. E 4. D 5. B

Parts of a Narrative Paragraph

A narrative paragraph has three parts. The first part is the topic sentence. The topic sentence is usually the first sentence. It tells readers what the paragraph is about and catches their attention.

The supporting sentences generally follow the topic sentence. They provide details explaining or supporting the topic sentence. The events of the story being told unfold in the supporting sentences.

At the end of a narrative paragraph, a sentence is needed to wrap up, or summarize, the ideas expressed in the paragraph. It brings the paragraph to a close and satisfies the readers' expectations. This is called the concluding sentence. It is usually a strong statement.

Read the following paragraph about Canada's first woman astronaut, Roberta Bondar. The topic sentence is shown in red in the paragraph. Can you tell which are the supporting and concluding sentences?

Roberta Bondar had been interested in space as far back as she could remember. At her home in Sault Ste. Marie, Ontario, she made plastic models of rockets and satellites. She and her sister Barbara built their own "space station" and pretended to be space travellers discovering strange planets. As Roberta grew older, she stopped playing such games, but she never lost her fascination with space. Someday, somehow, she was determined to get there.

Identifying the Parts

When Canada's first prime minister, Sir John A. Macdonald, was beginning his career in law, he worked for a lawyer by the name of George Mackenzie. John lived with George and his wife, Sarah.

John learned many lessons from George and Sarah. One of the lessons he learned was that it is important to be on time for work. John liked to sleep late in the mornings. He was sometimes late for work. One day, Sarah decided not to wake John. When he woke up, he realized that it was the end of the day, and he had missed an entire day's work. After that, John made sure that he was on time for work every day.

For more information on this notable Canadian, go to **www.cbc.ca/greatest/top_ten**, and click on "Sir John A. Macdonald." Write a brief paragraph about his life. Be sure to include a topic sentence, two or three supporting sentences telling about some of the events in his life, and a strong concluding sentence.

Creating a Timeline

Before writing a narrative paragraph, it helps to organize the events you are going to include. A timeline will help you do this. The events can be shown in the correct order on the organizer. For example, this timeline outlines key events in the life of Michaëlle Jean, Canada's 27th governor general.

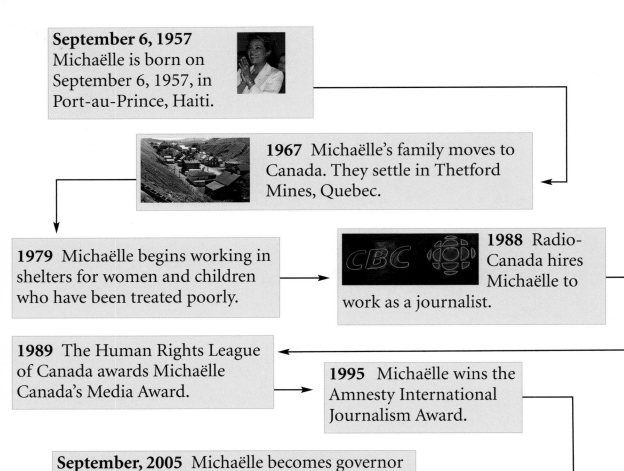

September 6, 1957
Michaëlle is born on September 6, 1957, in Port-au-Prince, Haiti.

1967 Michaëlle's family moves to Canada. They settle in Thetford Mines, Quebec.

1979 Michaëlle begins working in shelters for women and children who have been treated poorly.

1988 Radio-Canada hires Michaëlle to work as a journalist.

1989 The Human Rights League of Canada awards Michaëlle Canada's Media Award.

1995 Michaëlle wins the Amnesty International Journalism Award.

September, 2005 Michaëlle becomes governor general of Canada.

Think about the events in your life. The timeline of your life would include things that have happened from your birth to the present. Use photos and key events to make a timeline of your life.

Making the Sentences Flow

Lucy Maud Montgomery lived from 1847 to 1942 and has since become one of Canada's best-known writers. Lucy Maud grew up on Prince Edward Island. From a young age, she loved reading, telling stories, and writing. She began her career as a writer and editor for newspapers and magazines. She wrote romantic stories for women's magazines, but it was her novels that brought her fame. Her first and most popular novel is Anne of Green Gables, *published in 1908. Lucy Maud wrote seven other books about the character from the book—Anne Shirley. She also wrote other books, such as* The Story Girl *and* Jane of Lantern Hill. *Many of her books have been made into movies. Lucy Maud's books are enjoyed by people all over the world.*

Look at the pictures of Lucy Maud Montgomery on this page. Each picture is from a different time in Lucy Maud's life. Use the information at **www.lmmontgomery.ca** to write a timeline of the events in these photos. Be sure to include other key events in her life.

Understanding Unity

All of the sentences in a narrative paragraph should relate to the same topic. This is called unity. If a paragraph does not have unity, then one or more sentences do not relate to the main idea.

Read the following paragraph about Canadian **humanitarian** Craig Kielburger. All of the sentences are about Craig's public speaking skills.

At the age of 11, Craig entered his first public speaking competition. His speech was called "What It Means to Be a Winner." He was so nervous he forgot his speech. Instead, he made up a new one. He spoke from his heart, talking about the importance of fighting for what you believe in, even when there are obstacles. As Craig spoke, he became more confident. The audience applauded loudly after he was done. Craig won the gold medal. He entered and won several other public speaking contests.

Which Sentence Does Not Belong?

The following paragraph does not have unity. It includes a sentence that does not relate to the main topic. Find the sentence that is out of place in this narrative paragraph.

Canadian artist Emily Carr achieved success late in life. She created her best art after the age of 57. She would travel on sketching trips twice a year. Emily packed up her trailer with her pets and painting supplies. Then, she travelled to parks and forests to work on her art. Her first book was called Klee Wyck. She made many paintings on these trips. Finally, galleries wanted to show Emily's art. Her work appeared in cities across North America.

Emily travelled throughout British Columbia to find inspiration for her art. Where are some of the places you have visited? Write a narrative paragraph about a memorable event that happened on one of your trips. Make sure that all of the sentences in your paragraph relate to your topic.

Creating Coherence

The ideas in a paragraph should flow in a logical order from beginning to end. This is called coherence. Transitions can be used to create coherence in a paragraph.

The following paragraphs are about a **First Nations** woman named Thanadelthur. The paragraphs explain how she helped the Hudson's Bay Company expand the fur trade farther inland. Notice the transitions that create coherence.

In 1713, Thanadelthur, a Denesuline teenager, was captured by the Cree. With the help of some fur traders, she escaped and made her way to the York Factory trading post. There, Thanadelthur told the traders that the Denesuline wanted to trade furs with them. She also told the traders about the abundance of furs beyond the Churchill River.

The traders organized a voyage to map and explore the area. They asked Thanadelthur to act as their guide. The group embarked on a journey that took almost a year. During the journey, they were attacked by the Cree, but Thanadelthur convinced the Cree and Denesuline to make peace. Thanadelthur's role in the mission earned her the respect of both First Nations peoples and British fur traders.

Canada's history is full of interesting people who helped in the building of the country. Using the internet, research other historic figures, such as Samuel de Champlain and Nellie McClung. Find a person that interests you, and write a coherent paragraph about an event in that person's life.

Put These Sentences in Order

Before Jarome Iginla played for the Calgary Flames, he had to prove he could play well with the Kamloops Blazers. Can you figure out the correct order of the sentences to create a narrative paragraph with coherence? Look for clues to the correct order.

A. When the Blazers made the playoffs, Jarome began to play more often.

B. At first, the coaches did not give him much ice time. This is becuse they wanted Jarome to learn from more experienced players.

C. In his first year with the Blazers, Jarome scored nine points in 19 playoff games. This helped the Blazers win the 1994 Memorial Cup.

D. That year, the NHL's Dallas Stars **drafted** Jarome.

E. In 1993, Jarome moved to British Columbia to play for the Kamloops Blazers.

F. A few months later, he was traded to the Calgary Flames.

G. In 1995, Jarome and the Blazers won the Memorial Cup again.

Answers: 1. E 2. B 3. A 4. C 5. G 6. D 7. F

Tools for Paragraph Writing

What did you learn? Look at the questions in the "Skills" column. Compare them to the page number in the "Page" column. Refresh your memory about the content you learned during this part of the paragraph writing process by reading the "Content" column below.

SKILLS	CONTENT	PAGE
What is a narrative paragraph?	Pierre Elliott Trudeau, Frederick Banting	4–5
What are verbs?	Avril Lavigne, Jacques Villeneuve	6–7
How are transitions useful?	Margaret Atwood, Terry Fox	8–9
What are the parts of a narrative paragraph?	Roberta Bondar, Sir John A. Macdonald	10–11
How is a timeline useful?	Michaëlle Jean, Lucy Maud Montgomery	12–13
What is unity?	Craig Kielburger, Emily Carr	14–15
What is coherence?	Thanadelthur, Jarome Iginla	16–17

Practise Writing Different Types of Sentences

In Canada, Tommy Douglas is known as the "Father of Medicare." He campaigned for and won **universal health care** for all Canadians. His passion for health care may have been linked to an event that happened in his childhood.

Tommy was very sick when he was young. There was a bone infection in his leg that needed many operations. None of the operations helped him, and Tommy's family could not afford a specialist. When Tommy was 10, his doctor said he was going to have to remove Tommy's leg! Why? The doctor felt that it was the only way he could stop the infection from spreading to other parts of his body. Luckily for Tommy, a visiting surgeon agreed to operate on Tommy's leg for free. Tommy did not lose his leg after all.

Use the Internet, or visit the library to find out more information about Tommy Douglas. Then, write four narrative sentences about an event in his life. Try writing one of each of the following types of sentences.

In a telling sentence, the writer tells about something. This sentence ends with a period.

Asking sentences ask questions. They end with a question mark.

An exclaiming sentence shows emotion. It ends with an exclamation point.

Commanding sentences give direct orders. They end with a period.

Put Your Knowledge to Use

Put your knowledge of narrative paragraphs to use by writing about a person you consider a hero. The hero could be someone you know, someone famous, or someone you created out of your imagination. Remember that a narrative paragraph tells a story.

Ken Taylor is one of Canada's heroes. The paragraph below tells about an act of bravery he performed. Note that the paragraph has a topic sentence, supporting sentences, and a concluding sentence. The sentences flow in a logical order and are related to each other. There are many verbs throughout the text.

*In 1977, Ken Taylor was appointed the Canadian **ambassador** to Iran. Three years later, he became an international hero. In 1980, **revolutionaries** in Iran took over the United States embassy. They held 66 people hostage. Six American **diplomats** escaped from the hostage holders, but their lives were still in danger. Over the next few months, Taylor and another Canadian embassy official hid the six people in their homes in Iran. Then, with Taylor's help, the diplomats escaped the country. As soon as they were safe, Taylor closed down the Canadian embassy and left Iran as well. Taylor was called a hero. For his bravery, he was awarded both the Order of Canada and the U.S. Congressional Gold Medal.*

Choose one of the three people pictured below to research. Pick one event from their life that interests you. Before you begin to write your paragraph, make a timeline of the events. Begin with what happened first. Then, add what followed. End with the last thing that happened.

As you write your narrative paragraph, make sure that it has a topic sentence, supporting sentences, and a concluding sentence. Choose only sentences that relate to your topic. Finally, be sure that the ideas in your paragraph flow in a logical order from beginning to end. After writing your paragraph, identify the verbs you used. Can you replace some of the verbs with stronger ones?

Nelly Furtado

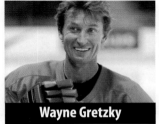
Wayne Gretzky

David Suzuki

EXPANDED CHECKLIST

Reread your paragraph, and make sure that you have all of the following.

- ✓ My paragraph has a topic sentence.
- ✓ My paragraph has supporting sentences.
- ✓ My paragraph has a concluding sentence.
- ✓ All of the sentences in my paragraph relate to the same topic.
- ✓ All of the ideas in my paragraph flow in a logical order.
- ✓ My paragraph has strong verbs.

Types of Paragraphs

Now, you have learned the tools for writing narrative paragraphs. You can use your knowledge of verbs, transitions, timelines, parts of a paragraph, unity, and coherence to write narrative paragraphs. There are three other types of paragraphs. You can use some of the same tools you learned in this book to write all types of paragraphs. The chart below shows other types of paragraphs and their key features.

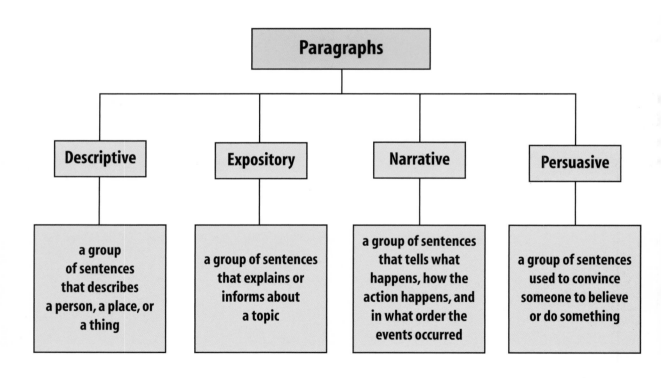

Paragraphs

Descriptive

a group of sentences that describes a person, a place, or a thing

Expository

a group of sentences that explains or informs about a topic

Narrative

a group of sentences that tells what happens, how the action happens, and in what order the events occurred

Persuasive

a group of sentences used to convince someone to believe or do something

Websites for Further Research

Many books and websites provide information on writing narrative paragraphs. To learn more about writing this type of paragraph, borrow books from the library, or surf the Internet.

To find out more about writing narrative paragraphs, type key words, such as "writing paragraphs," into the search field of your Web browser. There are many sites that teach about heroes. You can use these sites to practise writing narrative paragraphs. Begin by selecting one topic from the site. Read about the topic, and then use the checklist on page 21 to write a paragraph.

Visit *Canada's Sports Hall of Fame* to learn about Canadian athletes who have made great strides in their sport.
www.cshof.ca/hm_landing.php

The Greatest Canadian provides brief biographies of many Canadians who have achieved success in different areas of interest, such as science, entertainment, and politics.
www.cbc.ca/greatest

Glossary

ambassador: an official representative who represents his or her country in another country

contract: a written agreement

diabetes: a disease caused when the body is unable to absorb sugar and starch

diplomats: people who work for their government in other countries

draft: rough versions of books or other writings

drafted: selected to play on a team

First Nations: Canadian Aboriginal Peoples who are not Inuit or Métis

humanitarian: a person who is devoted to the welfare of other people

master's degree: a title given by a university to indicate that a person has graduated from an advanced study program

politician: a person who holds or seeks a government office

revolutionaries: people who support and participate in an uprising

universal health care: a program that provides medical care to all of a country's citizens

Index